$4.50 cloth
$2.50 paper

RICHARD DEUTCH

THE DIME

NEW RIVERS PRESS

New York
1970

Copyright © 1970 by Richard Deutch
Library of Congress Catalog Card Number: 76-139694
ISBN 0-912284-09-9
Cover by Neil Greenberg

Most of these poems, in one form or another,
have appeared in the following magazines:

THE NATION, THE QUARTERLY REVIEW OF LITERATURE,
THE POETRY BAG, PRISM INTERNATIONAL, THE ANN
ARBOR REVIEW, APPLE, THINGS, POETRY REVIEW TAMPA,
THE MINNESOTA REVIEW, INTERMISSION, THE TENNESSEE
POETRY JOURNAL, POETRY NORTHWEST, and THE SEVENTIES

Several of the shorter poems appeared as a pamphlet in THE OX
HEAD PRESS series, under the title of PRAYERS. Grateful thanks
are extended to Don Olsen for his permission to reprint them
and for his friendship and encouragement.

Ed Sweeney and Ed Niemeyer are the real translators of "Le Chat et
L'Oiseau," as the three of us know.

This book was manufactured in the United States for New
Rivers Press, P.O. Box 578, Cathedral Station, New York, New York
10025 in a first edition of 600 copies.

FOR YVONNE

CONTENTS

I. Love Poems and Prayers

II. The Dime

III. Voices of Hölderlin

I

LOVE POEMS AND PRAYERS

A Minor Sacrament

Walking last night in the woods,
I smelled your body. It was unmistakable,

And I stood in one of your presences
Surrounded by secret rituals

Of trees, rocks, weeds, dead
Snow. The evening

Paused for that moment,
An old priest forgetting his prayers:

The trees held their leafless postures,
Altar boys carrying candles,

And winter stood hushed in the vestibule.
This happened, and then it was gone.

Walking last night in the woods,
I smelled your body. Then evening started

To turn again, and I started for home,
The moon hung low in my path, like a flare

A Note

Since it is pretty well settled that we
are not going to sleep together,
and we have seen our separateness bloom
between us like a flower,

let us retire from the garden
and kneel down together without touching;
let us invoke the goddess
of diamond apples.

Then let us meet in a year
and speak of the sun going down
behind the fir trees;
of the ark of our self-possession,

how it possessed us.

To his wife

There is no one else
in the country of those who breathe
I love so much.

I will love you until my last breath
closes
into a first.

The cuckold's prayer

God,
give my anger.

There's another man
in her belly
and they speak my name
and they laugh at it.

The drunkard's prayer I

From the senseless smashing of objects
Lord, deliver me.

Her Tiffany lamp is
so delicate: —
and her tongue
delights in cinnamon.

The drunkard's prayer II

My body swims heavily
past the mirror,
a fish stares, disinterested,
out at me....

I'll sell you anything, even
the first six months of my birth.

Catullus XI

Furius and Aurelius, sworn to Catullus
were he off to the farthest Indies
or bound where Ionian waves
        beat up at the shore,

or were he to land in Hyrcania
or sport among golden Arabs,
daring Parthian arrows to venture
        where seven Niles color the waters,

or were he to cross the Alps
to see monuments of great Caesar,
or cross the remotest channel
        to the horrible Britons,

O sworn to Catullus through all of this,
carry these few lines to my mistress
and speak them as I have spoken them,
        none too nicely:

let her lay for her thousand lovers
and smear out her cunt to all of them,
loving none truly, but leaving
        them each one panting and dry:

but as for my love, let her not
count it hers, as once she could:
she has killed it herself, as a plow
slices the flower in passing.

Catullus LVIII

Caelius, our own Lesbia, that same Lesbia
Lesbia Lesbia the only one Catullus
ever loved more than himself
and all his brothers,
she's out in the streets and alleys
sucking the grandsons of great-hearted Remus.

Passer, deliciae meae puellae

Sorrow, how my girl loves you, she
plays with you and carries you
to her breast on her finger, teases you
to bite whenever she pleases,
she in whom my longing
is like a radiance

> (I think it soothes her thighs when
> Love inflames them):

O that I might play with you also,
easing heart's restiveness.

For S.

Moving beneath me,
we were a dance
at the world's edge;
a turning, a balance
"between wind that touches my fingers
& wind that touches the palm
of my hand."

It was not

worth it.
You have wasted my love for a lesson
learned too late.
I put down
the receiver,
my expression
lost.

Neither

Jealousy is
green all right

gangrene of the pullman washroom
on the train that takes you away

and night pours by
in section blocks

and the moon purrs
over the freightyards....

*

Jealousy is
green all right

translucent,
a pale liqueur —

it warms you, you
desire it,

you can "take it or
leave it alone," but you will

take it, glad of
the chance

Song: "One Autumn"

I fell in love
& talked about it

later I saw
a leaf the color of

Spring
& thought

Don't pluck it

In passing

Ellen,
if your hands were

flowers
I wouldn't

pluck them.
I would close

my hands
around them and feel

the swarms of glittering insects,
earth.

The Pet

This funny
little animal pain you
gave me
how I laugh to see it
follows me like my
shadow now &
doesn't even
cry all night
as it used to

A poem for Kadi

I love your sadness,
Kadi—
the sadness of lemon musk
staining your voice;
of animals leaving
the forest.

When I think of you, your long tendrils
reach out and draw me to you —
quiet as my long shadow
along your arm.

You turned your head once,
down the road;
you glanced at your shoulder,
and I thought that a bird
might be perched there.

And I thought of the empty chairs,
of the cigarette smoke, the people
dancing.

A Plea
(for Charlotte Moore)

There is no beauty in woman
that is not born
of silence.   Be
silent.   Sing
the blue pale song of the hyacinth
and the song of the clove and the marigold.

.

•

Anne Hexter

How shall I tell this child,
Whose hands are sparrows,
The wildness of her days
Or the dead sun's wrath?

*

Anne, the sun is dancing
In your arms.
There where you stand, it limes
The tongues of shadows.
Hyacinths
Deepen the evening.
The crickets
Are quiet, suddenly.

*

I hear the roses dying
In your veins.

To Ellen, When We Are Old

Outside,
In the drifting snowfall,
A girl walks naked.

Her feet barely press
The delicate
Stairways of snow.

I talked tonight with old friends,
Drinking,
Talking nervously,
Dying
For some way out.

Now I stand by the open window,
Watching the girl.
She moves in a prism.
Of silence. Her smile
Is a moonstone.
She cannot hear me.

Oh Ellen,
Ellen, dance me back
To the sea again!

Catullus again

beautiful
as snow that falls
in the sunlight

***

we lie
together

the vine
and the pale young juniper

***

my love for you
is the ivy that shelters
the oak
in the most ancient garden

The Necessity

Glorying in it, glorying
in necessity the mother of
love

we give what we must
spare
to one another

(it is
different
than we expected) What is

love but a
fading
stone

we ask
and dance together
among the leaves

Coming

She said she saw
the arabs scatter
and whirl
with a fury of birds
through the empty
streets of the town,
making for
the oasis.

Just before my
dawn exploded
I saw the river
winding east,
suspension bridge of
my dream
in the distance,
and knew for a minute
what that writhing
is for.

Spring

Things itch.

In my veins,
the red and white gloves
clapping time.

She walks
down the street
and her ass
is so happy to be one!

[Part of a much longer poem]

Tonight
　　my love
　　　　the rain is falling
from the fingers of leaves
　　in the heart's
　　　　dark forest
onto the roof
　　　　from the hands
(I told you
　　　　once
　　　　　　when you couldn't sleep
of the three serving women
　　　　in the house of Odysseus
how they wept
　　　　in their master's absence
wept
　　as they scattered the barley
onto the fire
　　　　to feed the usurpers
remember
　　　　I told you
　　　　　　how some god or other
pitied them
　　　　in their master's absence
pitied
　　　　a cold-bedded woman

a cowardly son
                        no good with words
pitied them
                        most of all their grief
and carried them
                        on a night like this one
into the sky
                        above the grey stormclouds
                                        knifing the sky
jagg'd as the bones
                        of old women
                                                and how their tears kept falling
into their hands
                        and dropped through their hands
                        on a world like this one
                                        My
love
        they continue to pour
                        their tears through their hands
on the fire
                        on a night like this one

autumn night/cafe on the rhine/apollinaire

My glass
is filled with wine
that shakes
like the flame of a match
in the wind

listen

somewhere a boatman is singing
his song about the night
and the seven women
who emerged from the river
their hair was blue
and long
enchanting the autumn
with their blue hair
and long

listen

the river is flowing
the people are dancing
and bringing me blonde-haired girls
with their coils of hair
and their silent gazes
listen
the river is flowing
the leaves fall in drunkenly
and follow

the yellow lights
shake in the river
like the flame of a match
in the wind

listen

the river is flowing
and like a rattle
the boatman's song   growing fainter

My glass is shattered like sudden laughter

Sudden Birds

Sudden birds in the forest —
A jangle of Bedouin dancers
Among the tentposts!

Socrates' prayer

O sweet god of the fields, and you other gods,
grant that the world be beautiful
inside me.

Song
(From the American Indian)

O great Sky-God,
don't you ever get tired
        of
the clouds between us?

In me

there is the image
of a lake, a pony grazing on the
gentle slope beside it,
a wooden raft.

We have travelled the dusty road
surrounded by cornfields,
and carried the ancient key
because it soothed us. We climbed
the wall,
good brick footholds and the red dust
scattered beneath us.

Now we have come to the place.
We lie down beside the lake
because we are here.

II

THE DIME

Scene from the Firemen's Picnic

The rain has left
a timid blue in the sky that's sore
from so much pouring;
and the green leaves
shudder raindrops
in the unfolding wind.
                    People move
solemnly through the wet grass
                    towards the huge
painted fireman, red and blue,
who rolls
his eyes and beckons.

Poem for the Question in the Throat

It's following me
It walks before me it walks too slowly
I pause and look down at its feet
I pause and look down at its feet

I am the man you suspected if only you knew me it would
        change everything
I killed Kennedy
I was behind the Bay of Pigs the senate race in New
        Hampshire the Miss America Pageant A.B.M.
        your
telephone bill
My voice is the noise of the cigarette machines

St. Louis Poem

"One evening an actor asked me to write a play for
an all-black cast. But what, exactly, is a black?
First of all, what's his color?"
—Genet

"No man should have that much power over so many."
-police captain, speaking
of Elijah Muhammed:
quoted in LIFE

The palm of the black man, raised
to face the enduring sun
grows out of the delicate wrist
of a St. Louis debutante,
stirring the water lilies
in the fountain of
Market Square.

Out in the thickets of Creve Coeur,
the bones of the slaves
are listening.

Two black cops, a german shepherd
poised like a guardian angel behind them,

sit parked on Delmar, awaiting
the rattle of chains with blue eyes.

Candy store

advertising
lovers' nuts

& chocolate-covered
cherries

Row on
row of

tinfoil hearts

agleam in my eyes in
the window —

*

Mother,
I have a yearning

for Bavarian mints,
for the wallets

of human skin.

Carried to Viet Nam while visiting the Jefferson Memorial Museum of History

(For Tom Connors)

1

It's frightening here

The headache ball is breaking the cornerstone of the Old
           Cathedral
inside they find
the corpse of the Indian strangely preserved
with a waxy coolness
three blackened kernels of maize
and a broken talisman of
red rawhide

2

The flag is torn

the flag which is waving blind to the sun of remorse

the pilot laughs as he sees the ruination of the herons
fall with the night the soft river
of the dying

his wake will strafe the beds of the wounded with lightning

American dreams dispersed in the dust of bullets
while Johnson dances with Billy Graham and Nixon dances
        with Truman,
their trousers rolled, in the burnt-out fields of the
        rice paddies....

The two fishermen

Once upon a time
there was a shrewd old fisherman
who bent down over the river,
his old eyes squinting like raisins
across the jangling coins of the water.
Every time he caught a fish
he laughed & laughed.
The eyes of the fish
were grey.

Once upon the same time
a pale young man in the moonlight
knelt on the banks of the river
as a forehead kneels
on the shore of its own deed.
Every time he caught a fish
he thought of the death
of the president.

The young draftee's prayer

Men
who are not my father
talk loudly while I am trying to sleep.

Academic Poem

That girl down the row
in Phil 203, a Radcliffe transfer,
doesn't believe in evil, knows
the Sophists didn't mean it. She toys
with her glasses.

                              I've seen
evil walking naked, unashamed,
transvestite Venus with pimples on her buttocks,
moving with heavy tread
across the waves.

For ————, Who Writes 3¼ Poems Daily

All things can tempt me to this craft of verse;
A pretty face, a coffee house, or worse,
The charm of being seen, though not of seeing:
For Beauty is my own excuse for being.

To C., An Actress

Because you discovered
who you are
and became her
and she is beautiful,

you cannot trust her
or yourself:

you love her,
but she frightens you
with her beauty.

Prince Privily I
(A Nursery Rhyme)

Prince Privily in self-defense
Went privily to bed
And privily, 'twixt royal sheets
Dispatched his maidenhead

In haste, lest Queen Bluntilda might
With soft insidious tread
Come lovingly, accusingly
to pat his royal head.

He'd spied once more the chambermaid
As she her mantle shed,
And all the proper passages
In John O'Hara read,

And lay now guilty, satisfied
Beneath the royal stain
That hardened to a royal crust
In blots that do remain.

Prince Privily II

lie in bed here
tossing &
sweating
Now it's got to be now
you've got to become a man
the king's son
                no more booze
                no touch self/hard
                cream

I am aware
that nothing will change
as I lie here
in the shapeless night,
that night hangs
like a thin ledge
over both of us.

The seminarian's prayer I

Once
I would like to know
the presence of God without having
to imagine it.

The seminarian's prayer II

if i died
you wouldn't be sorry enough
you bastard with your black cassock
& your blonde hair & your overfed stomach
you smiling dealer in poison & platitudes
Friar Lawrence, you bungler
Masochrist, you taught me to write
what i wasn't thinking &
wasn't writing
because your Truth wouldn't stretch to the edge
of what i thought
pay your goddamn surtax
then play golf all day
in a powder blue shirt with an alligator sewn on the
        pocket

49

& Father Dietz who used to throw stones
at stray dogs
& take walks in the woods with a stick to thrash the foliage

& Father Munie he tried to queer me

& Richard Sauget my friend he used to
cut himself with knives
to feel the sting of the disinfectant

& Patsy Gromacki i used to pour snow down her neck
to prove i loved her

you stupid bastard you taught me
your secrets

The snowflakes

do not fall:
back & forth

across my window and sometimes
at cross purposes,

they hesitate
on the wind that licks them

drily with her dry tongue.
I sit & watch the snowflakes

in a room that is mostly window,
trapped in my own commitment

to weather, sanity. They do not
remind me of anything.

But I think of a girl
I got drunk on once

and left, broke & maudlin, in a bar
on the lower West Side.

She was an easy lay, & I
a college kid on the make...still she

was younger.
Why did I leave her?

Remorse sprawls over my chest
like a drunken war buddy.

*

Why think of her now! why her
in the first place? Why,

of all places, here
in a room that is mostly window,

with only these snowflakes, cradled
outside by an unseen arm,

like nothing related to nothing,
continual changing, un-

able to change?

Reese

"I had a dog once, name of Reese
too. I paid four dollars for him,
had him only two years.

"Now when I think
of forty years
it's them two years I miss. It's that
goddamn four dollars."

Mrs. Reese

well
the front door come off in that big blow
waddled off like some drunk
or mebbe
like somebody'd wet his pants (minded me
of the day the twister uprooted dad
him all drunk an asleep
in the southeast pasture it liked t'carried him
off to Topeka
but no it set him down gentle
there where the brown stream bends toward the patch of
milo an he woke up an he smiled
a big fat pumpkin smile
an he got up an he dusted his hat off.

The Cat and The Bird
(After Jacques Prévert)

A grieving village hears
The song of a wounded bird
It is the only bird of the village
And it is the only cat of the village
Who has half-eaten the bird
And the bird stops singing
And the cat stops purring
And licking his paw
And the village gives
The bird a marvelous funeral
And the cat who is invited
Walks behind the little straw casket
Where the dead bird is laid out
Carried by a little girl
Who never stops crying
If I had known that this would make you feel so bad
Says the cat to her
I would have eaten all of him
And then I would have told you
That I had seen him fly away
Fly away to the end of the world
There where it is so far that
No one ever returns
You would have had less grief
Only sadness
And regrets

One should never do things
By halves

About Birds

What is it about birds, they are like poems,
Like stones pitched by a boy
In the direction of anywhere:

Yet somehow intelligent,
Rudely directive:
Forward: as if forward
Were anywhere,

As if anywhere were somewhere
For birds.

On a tombstone in Sicily

Traveller, do not laugh to see
this grave belongs to a dog.
I was wept for.

Wasp

Wasp, little warrior, trapped
between screen and window....

In flight, you thought yourself equal to anything.

In Belleville

I saw, for a minute,
an old man dusting his shoes,

swift rhythm of
his armstrokes

for a minute the same as the music
on my car-radio—

dusting of coaldust,
dusting of brickdust, dusting of

shoedust, as I
shot past—

The Dime

If I held a dime in the crook of the longest finger
of my left hand,
right where it meets the palm, and felt it
hard and silver against my hand's soft ocean,
and if I held it hard enough
and long enough,
it would leave a jagged impression
of some weak smile,
the hand's acceptance of
the day-long pain.

One Summer Night

The great sea of the crickets
Chirruped sullenly.

The turtle of sleep descended
On my chest.

I dreamt of a man, who climbed
The side of a mountain,
To reach the waterfall.
He drank, and was swept away.

Outside,
For a mile around me,
Nothing moved.

Morning

All night the sea came at us,
Carrying stars.
The dawn has risen in seashells.
The fisherman's wife, who rose
Before her husband,
Stands watching his skiff dissolve
Into the sun.

Before marriage

the lights across the river
nacreous
this windfall
evening I almost cried
at the touch of the snow.
she
is walking beside me, wearing
my pain
like a tattered hand-me-down,
says she would like to
sing me now
my hopes burnt out
to a house.

On hearing of the death of someone close to me
(W.K.)

Now is the time
to lower the eyelids
gently
onto the fists

Now is the time
for the funeral drum
of the heart
to swell without words

for the blood to rise
in the throat

for the forehead to kneel
on the shore of darkness and meteors

Now is the time
now is the time

Now is the time
for the lips and the hair
to touch ashes

Now is the time
for the heart to wade
to the beach of the moonlit island
behind the eyelids

Now is the time
to listen

only

the rush of the blood within
the hush of the air without

the husk of the man
between them

only the heart to stop them
keep them

Now is the time
to see through the eyelids
the air that is shaping
your face

On

　　entering Saks Fifth
　　Avenue the

colors are of a spring un-
known since Eden: icy oranges

purples pinks & greens The yellow
sun is streaking the

outraged palms of the mannikins,
tulips cluster

like spectators at an art exhibit
I go back in the street

　　& think of Poughkeepsie,
　　that savage art.

III

VOICES OF HÖLDERLIN

For Emanuel Deutch
In Memoriam
1911-1969

Hölderlin
(For Mary Chambers)

There are times when, driven and shattered,
    The heart retreats to the country
        Of hope, where superior wisdom
            Flourishes weapons in vain, bronze weapons in vain.

Home

The boatman steers home to the quiet
    waters with his harvest; and I too
        would return, but is my harvest
           only sorrow?

O forests of my youth, can you give me
    respite from too much love? you shores
        that suckled me, can you quiet
           my heart when I come seeking you?

Brevity

"Why are you so brief! Does your poetry
    matter so little now? In youth,
        in the days of hope, you found no
            end to your singing."

Joy was my song. When the sun has fallen
    westward, and the earth goes black with shadow,
        can you find their radiance? The bird
            of night whirrs fitfully past your eyes.

Youth

When I was a boy some god snatched
me away from the clamor, the passions of
men. Alone I ran
through the summer groves; with me only
the winds played.

And how the Sun my father used to fill
my heart with gladness! as if I were
a flower, arms outstretched, he
fathered me: and like Endymion
I possessed the moon.
                    If you could know,
you gods, my friends, how much I
loved you then!
                    I did not

know your names, as men call
"names," as if men
knew one another: but I knew

you far better than men. Stillness
of air I knew but not
the words of men.

*

Raised by the murmur of woods I learned
the silences of flowers. And I grew
in the arms of the gods.

Reminiscence

The northeast is rising,
dearest of winds for the promise
it bears, of stout hearts
and good sailing: Go,
wind, greet the Garonne, kiss
the gardens of Bordeaux, where the paths lead
along the stubborn shore, where the current
laps at the brook and the poplars
twine with the silver oak.

For my mind can see it: elm trees
reaching their huge fingers above the
housetops, playing in the wind; a figtree
alone in the courtyard. And on holidays,
brown women wandering the grasses; in March,
heavy over the paths, laden with
memories, the quiet breezes sing.

O give me that chalice, full
of the dusty light
that I may sleep
among shadows!

Sorry the man
who speaks without soul, the shades
of thought; good only to speak
the heart of words, the quiet burning song
of young days spent in love
and deeds fulfilled.

But what of
Bellarmin, what of his
companions? Many are those
who fear the spring, the
sea with its promise of wealth,
and knowing the earth
as painters of landscapes
know, they live alone,
under the leafless mast
where the night never breathes
its music or the sound
of strings, the people dancing.

The men are gone now,
bound for the Indies; and the Dordogne
pours down from the heavy hills,
and with it the huge Garonne where the current
swims. There is the sea,
robber and restorer of memory. Love alone
will hold our eyes. Yet all we
keep, all that endures, is the poet's task.

Ages of life
(For James Wright)

Cities on the Euphrates,
Streets of Palmyra,
Pillar-forests on the desert plain,
What are you?
When you left behind
The country of those who breathe,
The smoke and fire
Stole your heavenly crowns;
But I sit now under clouds (each
Has its own calm within)
And under a line of oak
On the deer's heath,
And strange to me, strange and dead
Seem the souls of the blessed.

The half of life

The land lulls in the sea, full
of summer, lapping yellow
pears and summer roses; swans
are gliding, drunk with love,
they kiss and gently dip
their heads in the sobering water.

When can I find, where can I find
when winter comes, the flowers? where
the sunshine and the earth's full
shadow?

       walls arise
cold and silent: in the wind
the banners flare.